Introduction

Take a look around your house. Chances are you have a roll of duct tape hidden under the sink, in a toolbox, or in a junk drawer somewhere. And if you don't, you should, because this book will take you through all the amazing things you can do with that simple roll!

Since I was a little girl, I've known about the amazing qualities of crafting with tape. It's clean, applies easily, and leaves no mess behind like paints and glues. For many years I happily used up roll after roll of clear packing and Scotch tape for scrapbooking and "laminating" all of my favorite pictures from magazines. I still enjoy a fresh roll of cellophane tape, but as years passed I learned about the power of duct.

Not only is duct tape strong enough to lift cars, build cannons, and fix engines, it's also cheap, easy to use, and lasts forever. And thanks to the wise Zen-like knowledge of duct tape aficionados spreading the word, you can now find duct tape in loads of colors, patterns, and finishes. With duct tape you get style and strength all in one—how can you beat that?

So read on to create some amazing belts, wallets, bags, and other accessories that will make even your favorite handyperson jealous. Chances are you'll find some idea you might have never thought of before, and you'll be unrolling the sticky stuff years down the road!

Happy crafting!

Choly Knight

ISBN 978-1-57421-895-4

Library of Congress Cataloging-in-Publication Data

Knight, Choly, author.
  Awesome duct tape projects / Choly Knight.
    pages cm
  Includes index.
  ISBN 978-1-57421-895-4
  1. Tape craft. 2. Duct tape. I. Title.
  TT869.7.K55 2014
  745.5--dc23
                2014027042

Acquisition editor: **Peg Couch** • Copy editor: **Colleen Dorsey**
Cover and layout designer: **Ashley Millhouse** Editor: **Katie Weeber**
Project photography: **Eric Forberger and Scott Kriner**
Step-by-step photography: **Matthew McClure**

© 2014 by Choly Knight and New Design Originals Corporation, www.d-originals.com, an imprint of Fox Chapel Publishing, 800-457-9112, 1970 Broad Street, East Petersburg, PA 17520.
Model photography on back cover and pages 3, 37, 39, 43–44, 46, 49, 51, 53, 55–56, 59, and 60–61 by Eric Forberger. All other project photography by Scott Kriner.

Printed in the United States of America
First printing

Contents

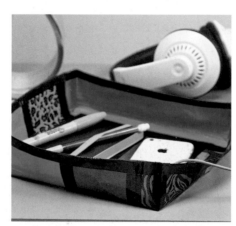

Idea Gallery

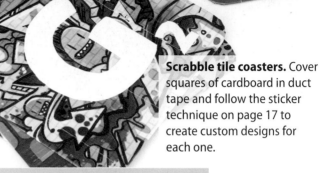

Message board. Use thin strips of colorful duct tape to separate a plain white dry erase board by day, class, project, or whatever works for you!

Scrabble tile coasters. Cover squares of cardboard in duct tape and follow the sticker technique on page 17 to create custom designs for each one.

Charging caddy. Cut an old bottle of lotion in half with an extension in the back. Cut a hole in the extension large enough for your charging plug, then wrap the whole package in duct tape; your phone now has a place to rest while it charges!

File holder. Save an old cereal box and cut off the top at an angle. Wrap the whole box in duct tape for a great place to store magazines, folders, or other important files.

Storage boxes. Breathe new life into old tins, boxes, and containers with some fashionable duct tape!

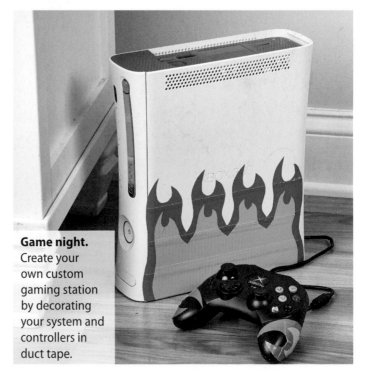

Game night. Create your own custom gaming station by decorating your system and controllers in duct tape.

Custom chucks. Create a stand-out sticker for your favorite sneakers.

Unique boots. Add a sticker or completely cover an old pair of boots to give them some flair.

Drawer organizer. Use up all those empty cardboard boxes. Arrange several small boxes in a way that fits your drawer. Cover each one in duct tape, and then attach them along the top and bottom.

Chain jewelry. Cut 3" (7.5cm) lengths of ¼" (0.5cm)-diameter cording and wrap each piece with duct tape. Connect the ends to form links. Join the links together as you make them to create chain jewelry pieces.

Sporting chance. Cover your favorite sports equipment in duct tape and give your team the edge.

Shoelaces. Fold a 1" (2.5cm)-wide strip of duct tape into thirds, then wrap another small strip around each end. When you finish, you'll have a perfect customizable shoelace!

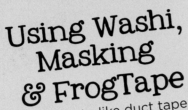

Using Washi, Masking & FrogTape

If you've gotten to like duct tape, you'll be happy to know there are lots of other craft tapes out there you can use to make amazing creations!

Washi tape is a tape made from Japanese washi paper, a decorative rice paper with a distinctive texture that looks beautiful and works well in crafts.

Masking tape, similar to duct tape, is an old standby that is now being manufactured in an array of colors. Most projects suitable for duct or washi tape could also be done with masking tape.

FrogTape is a recent invention that makes a huge improvement on old painter's tape. The adhesive, when moistened, forms a gel-like barrier that keeps paint from soaking through the tape. You can paint perfect, clean lines with it!

Decorate it!

Style your room, dorm, or home with these easy design ideas!

Instant abstract art. Put random strips of FrogTape all over a blank canvas. Paint each empty section in whatever colors you love. Then peel away the tape for easy abstract art!

Wall art. Cut a simple shape from a piece of foam core, and then cover it in washi tape for a personalized piece of art!

Paper lanterns. Paper lanterns are cheap and easy to cover with decorative washi tape. The result will give your room a charming ambience.

Cover a cutlery tray. Decorate a cutlery tray for a perfect spot to store cosmetics, stationery, or art supplies.

Revamp old boxes. Any old box can become new again with a layer of washi tape. This set of nesting boxes gets a new lease on life with lace and pastel tape.

Upcycle it!

Turn thrift store finds into treasures with the addition of decorative tape!

Jewelry. Add a layer of washi tape to old jewelry to give it a fresh new look!

Personalize it!

Show off your own personal style or just add a touch of flair to your favorite belongings!

Headphones. Show off your style while you rock out using some washi tape on your favorite headphones.

Screenprint a shirt. Apply a sheet of FrogTape to parchment paper like in the sticker technique on page 17. Cut out the shapes with a craft knife, and you have a perfect template for painting t-shirts!

Cords and chargers. With a bit of washi tape, you'll never get your chargers mixed up with anyone else's, and you'll know what goes where when they tangle up!

Sunglasses. Add some flair to classic black sunglasses with a few strips of washi tape down the sides.

Dog tags. Wrap military dog tags in a bit of washi tape to make a quick and easy statement.

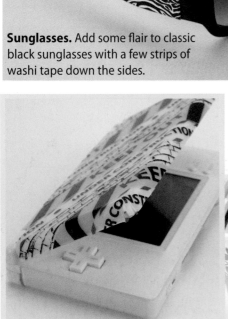

Gamer heaven. Cover your handheld gaming consoles in washi tape to make them stand out from the crowd.

Chopsticks and plastic bins. Use washi tape to make sure your lunch utensils never get mixed up with anyone else's, or as a labeling system for plastic bins to store craft supplies, jewelry, and other small treasures.

Organize it!

Take boring office supplies and make getting organized fun again!

Clothespins. Cover clothespins in washi tape and use them for hanging items on the wall and posting important reminders!

Tape magnets. Find a use for those business card magnets that businesses everywhere hand out. Cover them in washi tape and cut them into charming ripped tape shapes for use on your fridge.

Mint tins. Cover a mint tin in washi tape to store odds and ends and little treats for yourself.

Stationery set. Cover folders, notebooks, envelopes, pencils, clips, pen cups, and other stationery supplies in washi tape for an adorable matching set to give to yourself or friends!

Clipboards. Decorate clipboards in washi tape and hang them on your wall for a great way to stay organized.

Getting Started

The beauty of duct tape is that you need very little to get started creating! You can easily start working with just a simple roll of the silver stuff, but for the least headaches, there are a few more supplies that will make the unrolling more manageable. We'll also cover basic techniques to master so you can jump right into the projects!

The Essentials

Here are a few things you need to get started making projects that are as easy as they are professional looking.

Duct tape: The star of the show. Basic, plain-colored duct tape can be found in home supply stores, while colorful duct tape can be found at arts and crafts stores. If the selection you find leaves something to be desired, lots more can be found on the Internet as well.

Cutting mat: A gridded, cut-resistant mat is perfect for laying out strips of duct tape, allowing you to assemble sheets, shapes, strips, and more without getting adhesive all over yourself. The duct tape won't stick very strongly to the surface, so you can apply your project pieces and then peel everything off when you finish! An 18" x 24" (45.5 x 61cm) mat is a good size, although something as small as 12" x 12" (30.5 x 30.5cm) will still help.

Ruler: A sturdy ruler not only works well on its own with the shapes you'll be constructing, but also in conjunction with your craft knife. If you run the craft knife along the ruler, you'll get perfect straight cuts. A good plastic or metal ruler is suggested when using a craft knife, and if you can manage to get a quilting ruler, it will make measuring squares and rectangles a breeze. A size between 12"–18" (30.5–45.5cm) is perfect for what we're making here.

Craft knife: Duct tape can actually be ripped, but if you want clean, precise cuts, a craft knife is the way to go. Be careful with these, as they're extremely sharp. But with a fresh blade and a ruler, you can quickly slice through loads of duct tape while it's stuck to your mat.

Scissors: While you might get more use out of your craft blade than a pair of scissors while taping, you'll find that scissors are perfect for cutting those hard-to-reach places a craft knife just can't get to comfortably. They're especially helpful when you need to cut duct tape while the sticky surface is exposed—the scissor blades will slice right through the tape instead of dragging the adhesive. Your scissors will quickly get gunked up with adhesive when cutting duct tape, but it can be cleaned off periodically with Goo Gone or acetone nail polish remover. You could also invest in a pair of nonstick scissors. They're a bit more expensive, but if you love to duct, it would be a worthwhile investment.

ABOUT METRIC

Throughout this book, you'll notice that every measurement is accompanied by a metric equivalent. Inches are rounded off to the nearest half or whole centimeter unless precision is necessary.

CUTTING KIT

To get through most of the projects in this book you'll need your basic cutting kit. You'll see this referred to later in the projects.

- Cutting mat
- Ruler
- Craft knife
- Scissors

The Extras

If you really want to add some extra flair to your projects, these supplies will take you above and beyond.

Hook-and-loop tabs: Items like dots or tabs with a hook-and-loop surface are perfect for creating closures for your duct tape projects. Get the kind with an adhesive back (sometimes called the "no-sew" variety or hook-and-loop tape) and they're extremely easy to install. There's no fuss, and now you can make projects that open, close, and attach!

Zippers: If a hook-and-loop closure isn't quite what you're looking for, maybe you want a zipper. The fabric area of the zipper (called the tape) sometimes doesn't stick too well to duct tape adhesive, so additional reinforcement like staples or glue often helps. Aside from that, you can add it to projects like pouches and cases to lock your items up tight!

Staples: If your duct tape just isn't holding up like it should, a few staples can do a world of good. Use them on seams that are starting to split, a bag handle that needs extra strength, or when attaching a zipper. While it might seem crude, you can always cover up the staples with another piece of tape to keep the finished product looking polished.

Glue: Glue is ideal for sticking together areas where staples just can't reach. Just be sure you get a glue that is made for non-porous surfaces. Because duct tape is shiny and slick, ordinary craft glues might not work because they can't absorb into the tape.

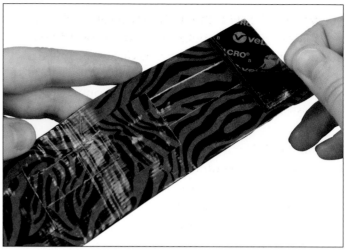

Apply both halves. The easiest way to attach a hook-and-loop tape closure is to leave the two halves stuck together. Then remove the backing from one half and apply the stack to your project.

Press the second half. Remove the backing from the other half and close your project, pressing the stack onto it. Now the two halves of the hook-and-loop tape will be applied to your project exactly where you need them.

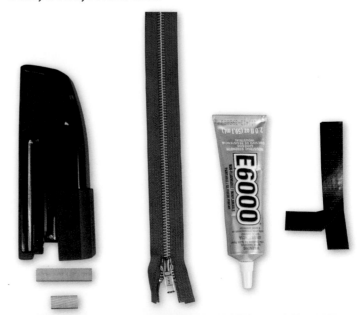

Closures. Supplies like hook-and-loop tape, zippers, staples, and glue work wonderfully to seal up your projects and add extra strength.

Brads: Kind of like the metal stud for duct tape, brads are incredibly helpful not only for adding support and strength to joined duct tape pieces, but for creating a bit of flash as well. Check out your craft store's scrapbooking section for brads that come in loads of shapes, colors, and finishes.

Cardboard: For some added structure and stability, a lot of projects in this book have a cardboard skeleton. This is where you can get creative! Cereal and food boxes, poster board, and cards are great sources of lightweight cardboard, while shipping boxes and mat board are great for projects that require heavy-duty cardboard.

Page protectors: Plastic page protectors or report covers make perfect clear sheeting in projects like frames or cases for touch-screen electronics. You could also use clear packing tape, but cutting up a page protector looks much cleaner, and they're incredibly inexpensive. Plus, if you're a student, you might already have some lying around!

Parchment paper: Just like your cutting mat, parchment paper is another surface that your tape won't stick to, so you can work on it without fear of the tape sticking where you don't want it. Unlike your cutting mat, however, parchment paper is traceable and transportable, meaning you can use it to make great decals and stickers for your projects! See page 17 for a quick tutorial on making stickers with parchment paper and duct tape.

Recycled materials. Scour your house to find these helpful items. Cardboard adds a wonderful sturdy structure to projects, page protectors create nice clear pockets, and parchment paper is perfect for stickers!

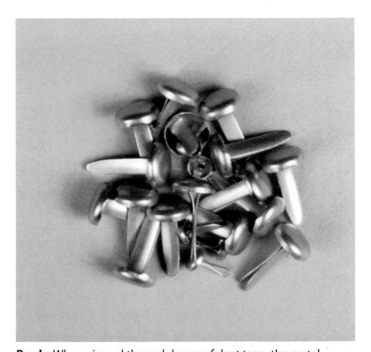

Brads. When pierced through layers of duct tape, the metal prongs of the brad are folded back to add extra strength, while the top part that remains exposed creates a polished look. Cover up the prongs with another bit of duct tape and your project can take much more wear and tear!

Basic Techniques

There are a handful of tried-and-true ways to deal with duct tape and get the best out of it. Once you have a handle on how these basic methods work, there will be no stopping you!

Creating a two-sided sheet

The most common kind of duct tape piece you'll need to make is a two-sided sheet. This method creates finished edges that are folded over so the whole piece looks polished.

STEP 1

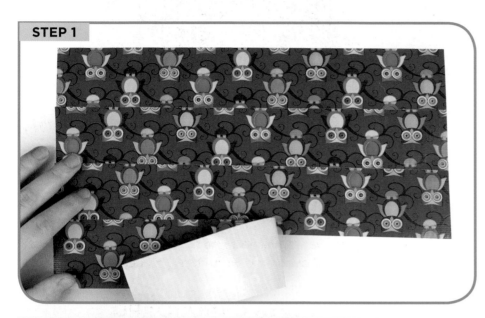

Layer the strips. Stick a strip of tape slightly longer than needed on your cutting mat (sticky side down). Overlap one long edge of the first strip by about ¼"–½" (0.5–1.5cm) with a second strip. Continue until you have a rectangle of tape slightly larger than required for your project. This will be the back of your sheet.

STEP 2

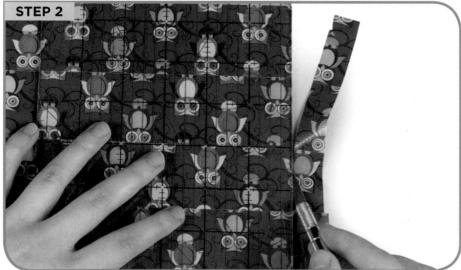

Trim the sheet. When all the strips are in place, trim the sheet so it's the exact size you need. Flip it over so the sticky side is facing up.

CREATING ROUNDED SHAPES

Follow Step 1 as before. For Step 2, trim your sheet to the shape you need with your scissors or craft knife. Then, in Step 4, make cuts in the sticky edges at even intervals before folding them over.

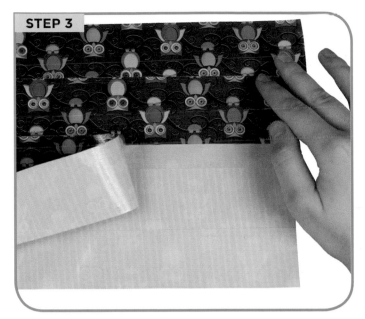

STEP 3

Cover the sheet. Apply strips of tape to the sticky side of the sheet just like in Step 1. Place the strips so they extend past the edges of the sheet by about ½″ (1.5cm) or so on all sides. This will be the front of your sheet.

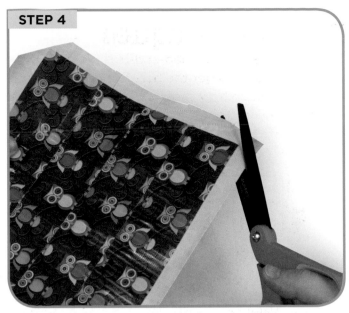

STEP 4

Trim the corners. Flip the sheet over so the back side is facing up. Using scissors, trim the corners of the exposed sticky portion, cutting close to the back corners without actually cutting into them. If you want to leave some sides cleanly cut instead of folded over, simply trim them off here.

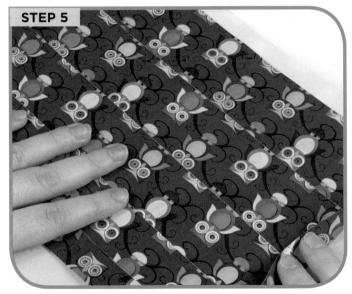

STEP 5

Fold over the edges. Fold over the exposed sticky edges to the back of the sheet to create a clean finish. If desired, you can use the sticky edges to attach your sheet to another piece instead of folding them over!

ADDING CARDBOARD

To give your sheet some extra thickness, cut a piece of cardboard to the exact size you need. In Step 1, cover the cardboard with tape on one side. Then, in Step 2, trim the excess tape from the edges of the cardboard. Follow Steps 3–5 as before.

Creating a box

This box shape is used more often than you might think in three-dimensional projects. Make a few using a cardboard skeleton and you'll have yourself completely organized in no time!

STEP 1

Make the base. For the bottom of your box, create a two-sided sheet as described on pages 14–15, making it the width (A) and length (B) you want for your box. You can add cardboard to the sheet or leave it out as you choose or as the project recommends.

STEP 2

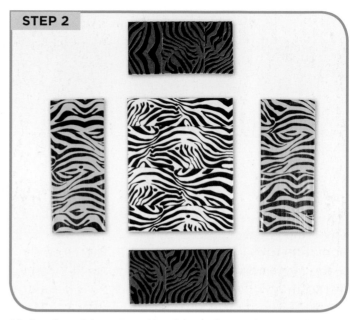

Make the sides. For the sides of your box, make four rectangles as wide as the desired height of your box (C). Two of the rectangles should be as long as the width of your box (A) and two should be as long as the length (B). You will have four side pieces total.

STEP 3

Attach the sides. Butt the edges of the box sides against the corresponding edges of the box base. Apply strips of tape over the places where the side pieces and base touch.

STEP 4

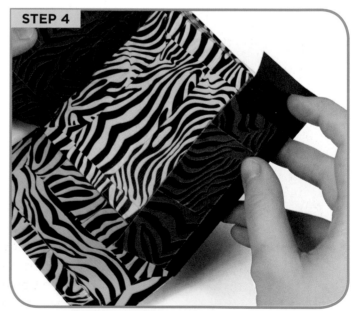

Fold the sides. Flip the box over and fold up the side pieces so the corners match up. Then tape the corners together to hold the box in place.

Creating a strap

The process for making straps is pretty simple on its own, but if you want to make them precise, the use of a quilting ruler makes it very easy!

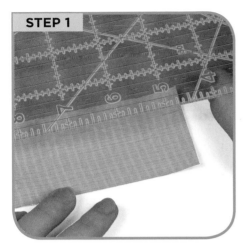

Apply the ruler. Lay out a length of duct tape on your mat, sticky side up. Place your quilting ruler on top of it so it overlaps one long edge by about ⅝" (1.5cm).

Fold the tape. Fold over the exposed edge of tape so it butts up against the edge of the quilting ruler.

Fold the remaining side. Remove the ruler, and then fold the exposed edge of tape over the strap toward the opposing fold.

Creating stickers

With a simple design and some parchment paper, you can create duct tape stickers to stick on anything!

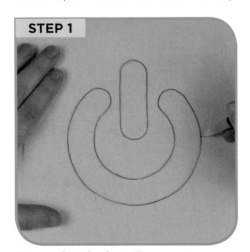

Trace the design. Trace your desired design onto parchment paper; the more visible the lines, the better.

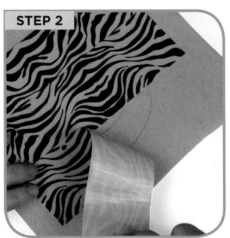

Apply the duct tape. Apply duct tape strips over the back side of the tracing, overlapping the strips until the design is entirely covered.

Cut the shapes. Follow the tracing lines on the parchment paper to cut out the shapes using scissors or a craft knife. To use the sticker, peel off the parchment paper and stick the shape wherever you like!

Sketchbook or Scrapbook

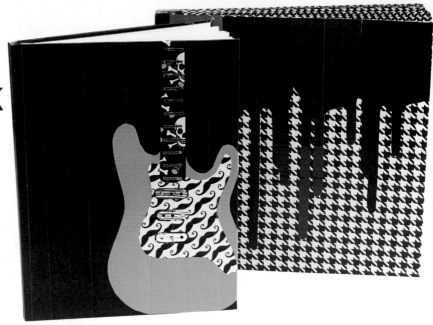

Makes: One book sized to fit the paper of your choice

Materials & Tools

- Duct tape
- Cutting kit (see page 11)
- Sheets of filler paper of your choosing
- Heavy cardboard: two squares ⅛" (0.3cm) wider and ¼" (0.5cm) longer than your paper sheets

Ever wanted to write your own book? Now you have the chance with this book-binding technique that requires nothing but duct tape! Make a homemade scrapbook with double-sided scrapbook paper, or create a sketchbook with your favorite drawing paper.

STEP 1

Start the first sheet. Take one sheet of paper and layer a strip of duct tape over the edge you want to be along the spine. Place the duct tape lengthwise along the edge so half of it extends out past the paper.

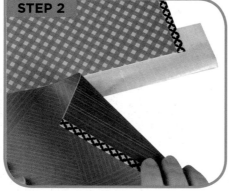

STEP 2

Apply the second sheet. Flip the paper over so the sticky side of the tape is up. Attach the next sheet, butting it against the first so it covers the exposed half of the tape. Trim any excess tape at the top and bottom.

STEP 3

Fold and repeat. Fold the pages in half along the center seam so the tape is on the inside. Repeat Steps 1–3 to continue creating sheets until you're happy with the amount.

STEP 4

Add the covers. Follow the instructions on pages 14–15 to cover the cardboard pieces with tape. Repeat Steps 1–3 to attach the front cover to the top sheet in the stack of paper. Attach the back cover to the bottom sheet in the stack. When finished, apply more strips of tape down the spine to cover it and help hold the cardboard pieces in place.

Tabletop Organizer

Makes: One box, 8″ wide, 8″ long, and 2″ tall (20.5 x 20.5 x 5cm)

Materials & Tools

- Duct tape in 3–4 colors plus a border color
- Cutting kit (see page 11)

We all tend to drop loose items like keys, spare change, headphones, chargers, and pens and pencils on the nearest desk, table, or nightstand when we enter a room. Why not create a real home for your things with this stylish organizer? Put it on an entryway table and you'll know exactly where to look for any missing items the next time you leave the house. Or, use it as a desk organizer to keep office supplies in a place where you can always find them.

Before you begin:

Follow the instructions on pages 14–15 to make six double-sided sheets in the following sizes: 3″ x 12″ (7.5 x 30cm), 3″ x 9″ (7.5 x 22.5cm), 3″ x 6″ (7.5 x 15cm), 3″ x 5″ (7.5 x 12.5cm), 3″ x 4″ (7.5 x 10cm), 6″ x 6″ (15 x 15cm).

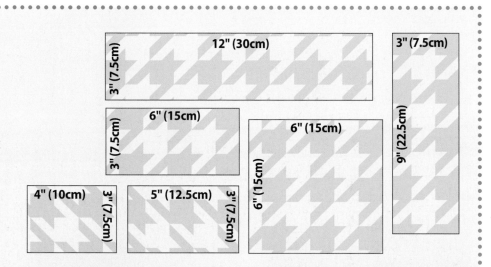

3″ (7.5cm) | 12″ (30cm) | 3″ (7.5cm)
3″ (7.5cm) | 6″ (15cm) | 6″ (15cm) | 9″ (22.5cm)
4″ (10cm) 3″ (7.5cm) | 5″ (12.5cm) 3″ (7.5cm) | 6″ (15cm)

STEP 1

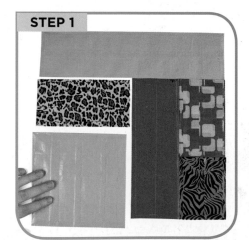

Arrange the sheets. Arrange the sheets as shown in the picture with all the back sides facing up. Butt the edges together as closely as possible, creating a 12″ x 12″ (30 x 30cm) square.

STEP 2

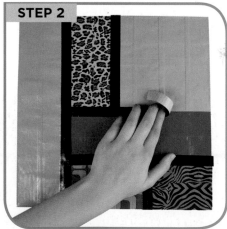

Attach the sheets. Cut several ½″ (1.5cm)-wide strips from your border duct tape and apply them over the places where the sheets touch. Flip the square over and repeat this on the other side. When finished, add borders around the outside edges as well.

STEP 3

Trim the corners. Cut 2″ (5cm) squares out of each corner. You now have a shape ready to make into a box as shown on page 16. Follow Step 4 for creating a box to fold and tape the sides.

CHARGING STATION

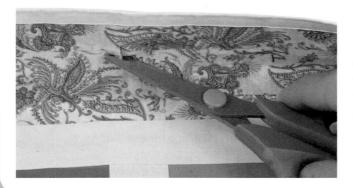

Cut + shaped slits in the back side of the box to accommodate your electronics while they charge. The holes will easily allow charging ports to slip in but not out!

Filmstrip Frame

Makes: One frame to fit four 4" x 6" (10 x 15cm) photos

If you have a collection of printed photos that you can't wait to show off, this frame is for you! With four slots, you can display a lot more memories!

Materials & Tools

- Duct tape in 1 color, plus white
- Cutting kit (see page 11)
- 18" x 8" (45.5 x 20.5cm) piece of cardboard
- Four 4" x 6" (10 x 15cm) pieces of report cover plastic
- Bone folder (or similar scoring tool)

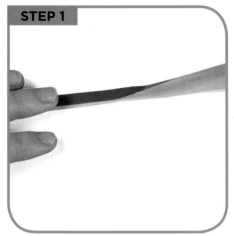

STEP 1

Finish the top edges. Fold a ½" (1.5cm)-wide strip of duct tape in half over one 4" (10cm) edge of each plastic rectangle.

STEP 2

Attach the sides. Place one plastic rectangle ½" (1.5cm) in from the right side and centered vertically on the frame base. Use ½" (1.5cm)-wide duct tape strips to secure both sides. Place the next rectangle ½" (1.5cm) away from the first and repeat, attaching the sides. Repeat to attach the remaining plastic rectangles.

STEP 3

Attach the bottom. Use a full width strip of duct tape to attach the bottom of the plastic rectangles. Overlap the bottom edge of the plastic with the tape by about ¼" (0.5cm). Then fold the edges of the tape over to the back.

STEP 4

Attach the decals. Cut several ½" (1.5cm)-wide strips of white duct tape and use them to create about forty-eight ½" (1.5cm) white squares. Apply the squares along the top and bottom edges of the frame, spaced about ¼" (0.5cm) apart.

Before you begin:

Measure and score the cardboard rectangle at 4½″, 9″, and 13½″ (11.5, 23, and 34.5cm) from one short side as shown. Then, refer to the two-sided duct tape sheet technique on page 14–15 to cover both sides with tape.

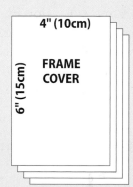

18″ (45.5cm)

FRAME BASE

4″ (10cm)

FRAME COVER

6″ (15cm)

8″ (20.5cm)

MOUNTAIN FOLD

VALLEY FOLD

MOUNTAIN FOLD

4½″ (11.5cm)   4½″ (11.5cm)   4½″ (11.5cm)   4½″ (11.5cm)

Book Cover

Makes:
One cover, sized to fit your book

Materials & Tools
- Duct tape
- Cutting kit (see page 11)

If you've got to protect your books from scratches and wear, you might as well do it with class, right? Make an eye-catching and sturdy book cover by using fashionable and tough duct tape!

Measure your book

Measure the different parts of your book to get a cover that fits just right: cover length (A), cover width (B), book width (C).

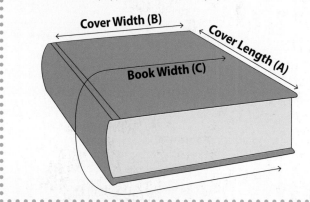

Cut the pieces

Follow the instructions on pages 14–15 to create a double-sided sheet equal to B + C by A.

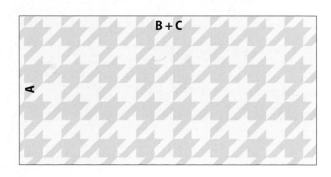

STEP 1

Fold the ends. Divide B by 2. Then, measure in this amount from each short end and make a mark. Fold the short ends over, aligning the folds with the marks.

STEP 2

Tape the edges. Tape the folds in place by applying strips of tape along the bottom and top edges. Slip your book cover into these pockets to complete your look! Add some stickers or a pencil pocket for a finishing touch.

PENCIL POCKET

Tape a 4" x 5" (10 x 12.5cm) two-sided sheet to the front of your book for the perfect pencil pocket! Remember to only tape along the sides and bottom of your pocket piece, leaving the top edge untaped.

Wallet Smartphone Case

Makes:
One wallet/case to fit most 2½" x 4½"–5" (6.5 x 11.5–12.5cm) phones

Materials & Tools
- Duct tape
- Cutting kit (see page 11)
- Two 3¾" x 6¼" (9.5 x 16cm) cardboard pieces
- 3¼" x 5¾" (8.5 x 14.5cm) piece of report cover plastic
- ½" (1.5cm) of adhesive-backed hook-and-loop tape

Why carry around clunky bags and purses when what most of us need is a place for our phone and credit cards? Get both in one with this sleek wallet and phone case combo!

Before you begin:

Follow the instructions on pages 14–15 to create four 3¼" x 3" (8.5 x 7.5cm) two-sided sheets. Follow the instructions on page 17 to create a 2" x ⅝" (5 x 1.5cm) strap. Trim two adjacent corners on the long edges of the outer case cardboard pieces so they are rounded.

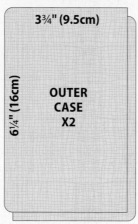

3¾" (9.5cm)
6¼" (16cm)
OUTER CASE X2

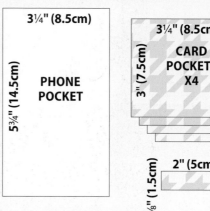

3¼" (8.5cm)
5¾" (14.5cm)
PHONE POCKET

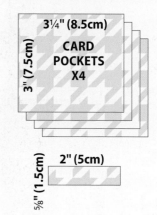

3¼" (8.5cm)
3" (7.5cm)
CARD POCKETS X4

⅝" (1.5cm) 2" (5cm)

STEP 1

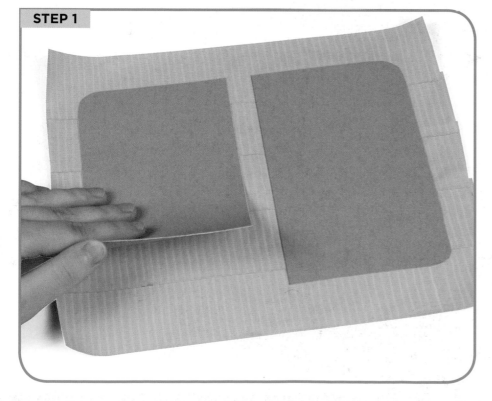

Cover the outer case. Layer strips of tape together to create a one-sided sheet about 10" x 8" (25.5 x 20.5cm). Place the cardboard pieces on the sticky side about ⅝" (1.5cm) apart (for the spine). Make sure the pieces mirror one another with the rounded corners at the outside. Following the instructions on pages 14–15, trim the excess tape around the edges, cover the other side of the cardboard with tape, trim the corners, and fold over the edges.

STEP 2

Add the strap. Center one end of the strap along the right edge of the case, and tape it in place on the inside of the case.

STEP 3

Edge the phone pocket. Fold a ½" (1.5cm)-wide strip of duct tape in half over one short end of your phone pocket.

STEP 4

Attach the phone pocket. Center the pocket on the inside of the case on the right side. Then use ½" (1.5cm)-wide strips of tape to secure the pocket along the sides and bottom.

STEP 5

Attach the card pockets. Center one card pocket on the inside of the case on the left side, ¾" (2cm) down from the top edge. Tape the pocket in place along the bottom edge only.

STEP 6

Add the remaining pockets. Attach the next card pocket ½" (1.5cm) down from the first, only taping along the bottom edge. Continue with the remaining two pockets. When finished, you will have a staggered stack of pockets. Apply strips of tape to both sides of the stack to secure..

STEP 7

Finish. Decorate the outside of the case as desired with stickers or other embellishments. To finish, attach one half of the hook-and-loop tape to the end of the strap. Attach the the other half to the front side of the case.

MINI-LESSON: WEAVING

Weaving is a classic technique that you can do with strips of duct tape. The length and width of the strips you choose will ultimately determine the size of your finished woven block, so you can use weaving in lots of other projects in this book, such as the Flip-Flops on page 54. To make a woven version of the smartphone case, create the following double sided strips: Eleven ¾" x 6⅜" (2 x 16cm) strips and seven ¾" x 9" (2 x 23cm) strips.

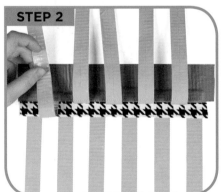

STEP 1

Arrange your vertical strips. Follow the instructions on page 17 to create strips for weaving. Arrange the vertical strips in a row so the long edges touch and the top ends are completely even. Temporarily tape the strips in place along the top to keep them from moving as you work.

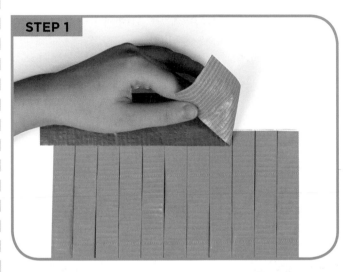

STEP 2

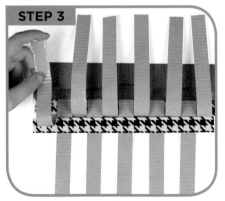

STEP 3

STEP 4

Flip back the strips. Starting with the second from right strip, flip back every other vertical strip in the configuration, and then place a horizontal strip over the remaining vertical strips.

Flip down the strips. Flip the vertical strips back down over the horizontal strip you just added. Repeat Step 2, but start with the far right strip. You should be flipping back all the strips that weren't flipped before. Add a new horizontal strip. Repeat Steps 2 and 3 until you reach the bottom of the vertical strips.

Finish the edges. To finish the edges of your woven piece so it doesn't come undone, fold a ½" (1.5cm)-wide strip of duct tape in half over each edge.

Tablet Case

Makes: One 8" x 10" (20.5 x 25.5cm) case

Materials & Tools

- Duct tape in 1–2 colors
- Cutting kit (see page 11)
- ⅓ yd. (33cm) fleece fabric
- 4" (10cm) of adhesive-backed hook-and-loop tape

If you're a student, chances are your tablet is one of the most valuable things you own. Made from soft and padded fleece fabric, this case will keep it nice and safe. There's even a pocket in the back for your charging cord—extra practical!

STEP 1

Add the back pocket. Place the back pocket on top of the back piece, aligning the bottom edges. Both pieces should be tape side up. Tape the pocket in place along the sides and bottom.

STEP 2

Add the back flap. Place the back flap on top of the back piece, centering it 1" (2.5cm) above the back pocket. Tape the flap in place along the bottom edge only. Consider taping along both sides of the bottom edge for extra security.

STEP 3

Add the front. Place the back piece fleece side up. Place the front piece on top of it, fleece side down, aligning the sides and bottom edges. Tape the front piece in place along the sides and bottom edges.

STEP 4

Apply the hook-and-loop tape. Cut the hook-and-loop tape into two 2" (5cm)-long pieces. Attach the hook side to the fleece side of the back flap, centered about ⅜" (1cm) from the edge. Attach the loop side to the case front, centered about 1" (2.5cm) from the top edge.

Before you begin:

Cut your fleece into the following pieces: back 11" x 10" (28 x 25.5cm), front 10" x 8" (25.5 x 20.5cm), back pocket 10" x 6" (25.5 x 15cm), back flap 9" x 2" (23 x 5cm). Follow the instructions on pages 14–15 to cover ONE side of each piece with tape (following Steps 3–5).

Takeout Lunch Box

Makes:
One 6" x 6" x 6" (15 x 15 x 15cm) box

Materials & Tools
- Duct tape in 1–2 colors
- Cutting kit (see page 11)
- Cardboard pieces:
  - Bottom: One 5" x 5" (12.5 x 12.5cm)
  - Sides: Four 6" x 6" (15 x 15cm)
  - Top Flaps: Two 5½" x 6" (14 x 15cm)
  - Side Flaps: Two 3" x 6" (7.5 x 15cm)
- 1" (2.5cm) of adhesive-backed hook-and-loop tape
- Two brads

Add a little bit of flair to your lunch with this eye-catching lunch box. Whether you're stowing away Chinese leftovers or homemade goodies, this box will completely reinvent the way you brown bag it!

STEP 1

Create the box. Follow the instructions on page 16 to create a box from the bottom and side pieces. Attach the sides to the bottom, and then fold the sides up and tape the corners together.

STEP 2

Add the flaps. Add the two side flaps by taping them to the top edge of opposing sides of the box. These will barely come together in the middle. Add the two top flaps to the remaining opposing sides of the box; these should overlap in the middle.

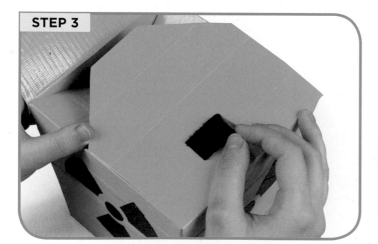

STEP 3

Attach the hook-and-loop tape. Apply the hook side of the hook-and-loop tape to the underside of one of the top flaps, centered ¼" (0.5cm) down from the top edge. Press the loop half in place on the top side of the other top flap using the technique on page 12.

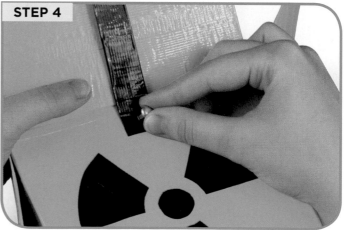

STEP 4

Attach the strap. Position one end of the strap centered about 1" (2.5cm) down from the bottom of one of the side flaps. Secure it with a brad (you can use an awl, hole punch, or craft knife to make the hole). Repeat on the opposite side of the box with the other end of the strap. Cover the prongs of the brads on the inside of the box with tape.

Before you begin:

Trim the corners of the cardboard pieces as shown. Refer to the two-sided duct tape sheet technique on pages 14–15 to cover both sides of all the cardboard pieces with tape. Follow the instructions on page 17 to create a 15" (38cm)-long strap of duct tape for the handle.

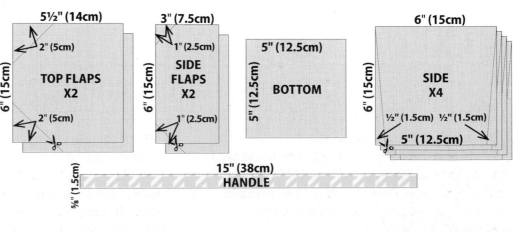

5½" (14cm)

2" (5cm)

6" (15cm)

TOP FLAPS X2

2" (5cm)

3" (7.5cm)

1" (2.5cm)

6" (15cm)

SIDE FLAPS X2

1" (2.5cm)

5" (12.5cm)

5" (12.5cm)

BOTTOM

6" (15cm)

6" (15cm)

SIDE X4

½" (1.5cm)   ½" (1.5cm)

5" (12.5cm)

⅝" (1.5cm)

15" (38cm)

HANDLE

ID Holder with Strap

Makes:

One 3" x 4½" (7.5 x 11.5cm) holder to fit most ID cards

Materials & Tools

- Duct tape
- Cutting kit (see page 11)
- 3" x 4½" (7.5 x 11.5cm) piece of cardboard
- 2½" x 3¾" (6.5 x 9.5cm) piece of report cover plastic
- One brad

A re you making a quick trip to the gym and want to travel light? Or maybe you just want to have a unique badge for work, school, or events. Either way, this handy holder is a perfect fit. Make it for your wrist or long enough to wear around your neck—your ID or badge will be safe and secure. Remember to complete the steps in the Before you begin section on the next page before proceeding to Step 1.

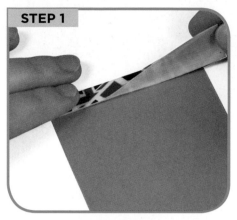

STEP 1

Edge the badge pocket. Fold a ½" (1.5cm)-wide strip of duct tape in half over one short end of your pocket piece.

STEP 2

Apply the pocket. Center the pocket on top of the base, aligning the bottom edges. Then tape it in place along the sides and bottom using ½" (1.5cm)-wide strips of duct tape.

STEP 3

Cut a hole for the strap. Using your craft knife, cut a rectangular hole measuring ⅛" x ¾" (0.3 x 2cm) about ¼" (0.5cm) down from the top edge of the holder.

STEP 4

Attach the strap. Loop the strap through the hole in the base and secure the ends with duct tape. Install a brad going through the strap for more security, and then cover the exposed prongs on the back side with more duct tape.

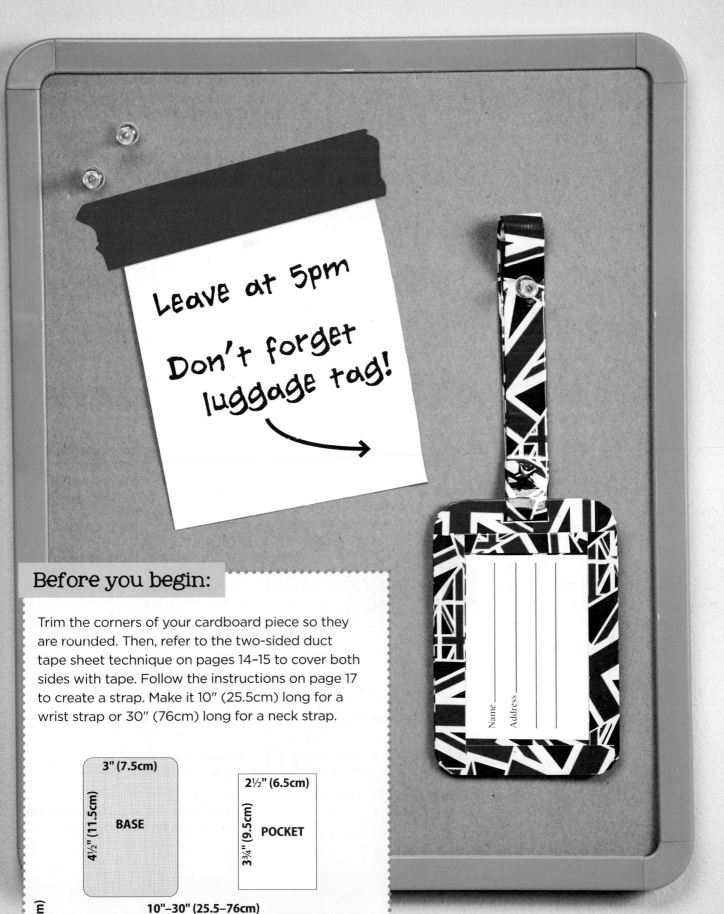

Leave at 5pm

Don't forget luggage tag!

Before you begin:

Trim the corners of your cardboard piece so they are rounded. Then, refer to the two-sided duct tape sheet technique on pages 14–15 to cover both sides with tape. Follow the instructions on page 17 to create a strap. Make it 10" (25.5cm) long for a wrist strap or 30" (76cm) long for a neck strap.

3" (7.5cm)

4½" (11.5cm)

BASE

2½" (6.5cm)

3¾" (9.5cm)

POCKET

10"–30" (25.5–76cm)

⅝" (1.5cm)

STRAP

Name

Address

Watch Cuff

Makes: One cuff-style watch sized to fit your watch face and wrist

Materials & Tools
- Duct tape
- Cutting kit (see page 11)
- Watch face with vertical slots for attaching to cuff
- 3½" (9cm) of adhesive-backed hook-and-loop tape
- 4–8 brads

Make your watch into a true statement piece with this large, bold design. Here you can make the perfect cuff to match a watch face of your choosing, and people will get a glance at your sense of style right away!

STEP 1

Create the watch tabs. Follow the instructions on pages 14–15 to create two double-sided rectangles that are 2" (5cm) long and wide enough to fit into the slots of your watch face.

STEP 2

Place the watch face. Wrap the tabs you made in Step 1 around the slots in your watch face. Then center the watch face along your watch strap.

STEP 3

Install the brads. Using your craft knife, install the brads going through all the layers of the tabs and strap. Depending on the size of your watch, you can use one large brad or several small brads as shown. Cover the exposed prongs on the back side with tape.

STEP 4

Attach the hook-and-loop tape. Cut the hook-and-loop tape to fit the width of your watch strap. Attach the hook piece to one end of the strap on the front side. Then add the loop piece to the other end of the strap on the back side.

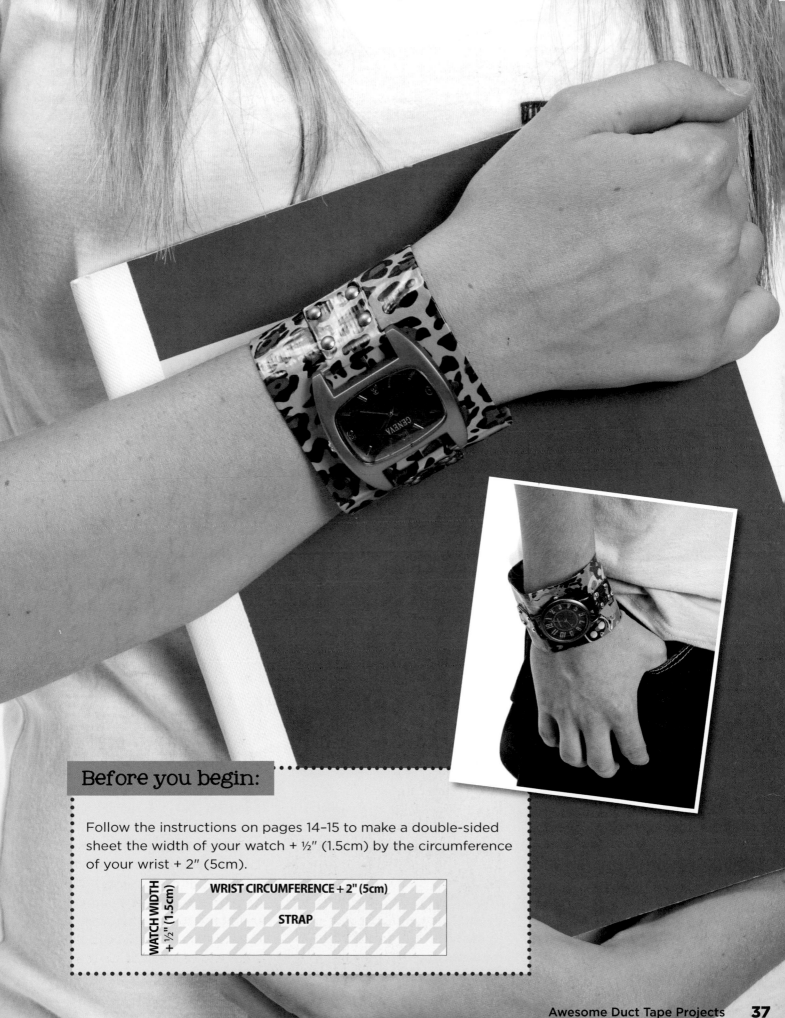

Before you begin:

Follow the instructions on pages 14–15 to make a double-sided sheet the width of your watch + ½″ (1.5cm) by the circumference of your wrist + 2″ (5cm).

WATCH WIDTH + ½″ (1.5cm)

WRIST CIRCUMFERENCE + 2″ (5cm)

STRAP

Belt Utility Pouch

Makes: One 3½" x 5"
(9 x 12.5cm) pouch

Materials & Tools
- Duct tape
- Cutting kit (see page 11)
- 1½" (4cm) of adhesive-backed hook-and-loop tape

Are you the kind of person who always has your phone, notebook, or multi-tool on hand? Then this pouch will work perfectly with your style. It fits nicely on your belt and will snugly carry anything you need to have at arm's reach.

STEP 1

Attach the pocket. Center the pocket on top of the back piece, aligning the bottom edges. Then tape it in place along the sides and bottom.

STEP 2

Apply the hook-and-loop tape. Cut a 1" (2.5cm) strip of hook-and-loop tape. Attach the hook side centered ½" (1.5cm) down from the top edge of the back piece. Attach the loop side centered ½" (1.5cm) down from the top edge of the pocket.

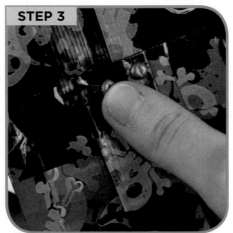

STEP 3

Add the belt strap. Flip the pouch over so you are working on the back side. Tape one end of the strap centered about 2¼" (5.5cm) down from the top edge. Make sure the end is pointing up toward the top of the pouch as shown. Add brads as desired for extra security, remembering to cover the prongs with tape when finished.

STEP 4

Apply hook-and-loop tape to the strap. Take the remaining ½" (1.5cm) strip of hook-and-loop tape and apply the hook half to the free end of the strap on the underside. Press the loop half in place on the back of the pouch using the technique on page 12.

Before you begin:

Follow the instructions on pages 14–15 to make three double-sided sheets in the following sizes: 3 ½" x 5" (9 x 12.5cm), 3½" x 7" (9 x 17.5cm), 1" x 4 ½" (2.5 x 11.5cm).

3½" (9cm)

BACK

7" (17.5)

3½" (9cm)

POCKET

5" (12.5cm)

1" (2.5cm)

STRAP

4½" (11.5cm)

Flowers

Makes:

One flower any size

Materials & Tools

- Duct tape
- Cutting kit (see page 11)
- Pen, pencil, or chopstick for stem

Flowers are a classic duct tape project, but you'd be surprised to see how easy it is to design your own! Create completely unique flowers with these simple tips and techniques!

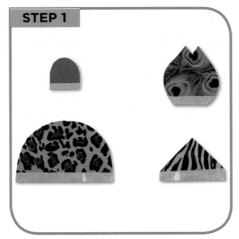

STEP 1

Create the petals. Create double-sided strips of duct tape, leaving ¼" (0.5cm) of the sticky side of the tape exposed along the bottom edge. Cut these strips into petal shapes of your own design. Here are some ideas. You'll need about 20–50 petals depending on the size of flower you want.

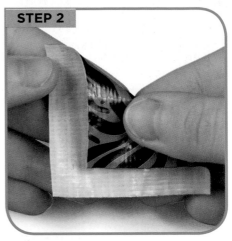

STEP 2

Create a pointed petal. To create a pointed petal, start with a 2" x 2" (5 x 5cm) square of duct tape. Fold the upper right corner down toward the bottom left corner, leaving ¼" (0.5cm) of the sticky side of the tape exposed along the bottom edge.

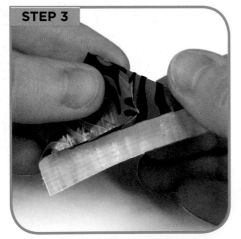

STEP 3

Finish the pointed petal. Fold the upper left corner down toward the bottom right corner so the edges of the folded pieces align. This creates a triangle with a ¼" (0.5cm) sticky extension along the bottom.

STEP 4

Attach to the stem. Select a stem for your flower. This can be a pencil, pen, or other object covered in duct tape. Wrap the first petal completely around the stem, covering the tip. The sticky side of the tape left exposed will hold the petal in place.

STEP 5

Form the inner petals. Apply the inner petals, wrapping them around the original one. Attach each petal slightly higher than the previous one to get a blooming effect.

STEP 6

Form the outer petals. Continue adding petals until the flower reaches the size you want. When complete, pointed green petals can be added around the base of the flower as leaves.

Prom Bodice & Vest

Makes:
One duct tape covered bodice or vest

Materials & Tools
- Duct tape
- Cutting kit (see page 11)
- For bodice:
  - Comfortable close-fitting tank top
  - Separating zipper equal to the length of your tank top
  - A friend or dress form (see step 1)
  - Stapler
- For vest:
  - Vest
  - About 20" (51cm) of thin gauge jewelry wire

Ever thought about taking on the Duct Tape Prom Outfit Challenge? Win and you could earn a scholarship for you and your date! There's no denying that it's called a challenge for a reason, but with the tips and tricks here, you'll be more than ready to tackle the tape. I'll take you step by step through making a bodice and a vest, but you can apply these techniques to pants, skirts, and jackets as well.

For the bodice:

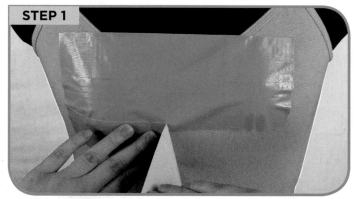

STEP 1

Cover the bust. Wear the tank top while a friend applies tape, or use a dress form. For best coverage, you're aiming for a result that's something like a corset. Apply strips of tape going horizontally across the upper chest and bust. Repeat this with a few strips on the back. Then join the front and back sections with a few strips at the sides.

STEP 2

Create the strap. If you want a strap for your bodice, create one now using the two-sided sheet technique (pages 14–15). Attach it to the bust and back of your bodice with more tape.

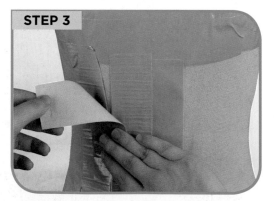

STEP 3

Cover the torso. Cover the torso area of the bodice with vertical strips of duct tape that are perpendicular to the ground. Depending on how curvy you are, you will end up with triangle-shaped gaps—simply cover them up with more pieces of tape.

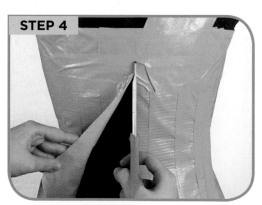

STEP 4

Cut the bodice. Have your friend cut you out of the top, cutting right up the center of the back. Be very careful during this step.

For the bodice: (continued)

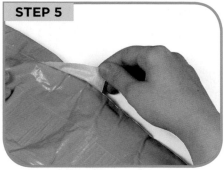

Trim the edges. Fold strips of tape in half over the top and bottom edges, as well as the cut edges, of the bodice to finish them up and make them look neat and clean.

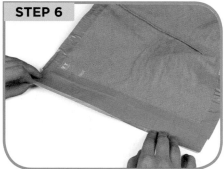

Create extensions. If you need to add some breathing room to your bodice so it's not quite so tight, layer more tape along the cut edges and then fold the tape over as shown. Adding ½″–1″ (1.5–2.5cm) on each side usually does the trick.

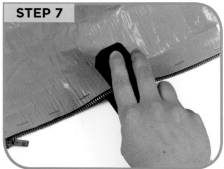

Staple the zipper. Apply each side of the zipper to the center back opening of the bodice with staples. Cover the exposed staples with more duct tape when complete.

For the vest:

STEP 1

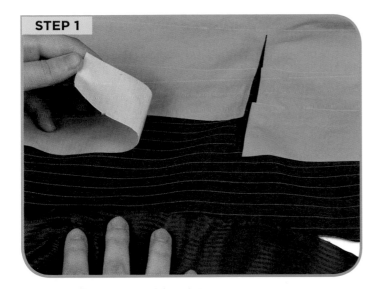

Cover the fabric. Using scissors, remove the buttons from your vest and set them aside. Cover the outside of the vest with overlapping vertical strips of tape. Place the tape so it extends 1″ (2.5cm) past the top and bottom edges of the vest. Then, fold these ends over to the back of the vest.

STEP 2

Cover the buttons. Loop a bit of wire through one of the buttons. Then cover the button using a circle of duct tape. Twist the wire several times to create a shank for the button. Repeat with the remaining buttons.

STEP 3

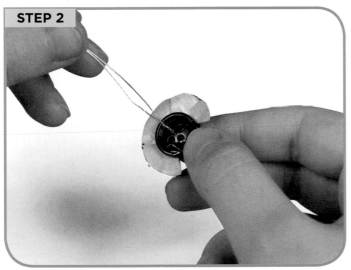

Install the buttons. Poke the wire through the vest where the button was sewn before. Trim the wire and bend it flat against the vest. Tape it in place to secure it and cover the wire ends. Repeat with the remaining buttons. To finish, cut open the previous buttonholes in the vest.

Necktie & Bow Tie

Makes:
One necktie or bow tie

Materials & Tools
- Duct tape
- Cutting kit (see page 11)
- Hair clip or ½" (1.5cm) strip of hook-and-loop tape

While you could make a tie by simply covering an old one you have on hand in duct tape, just like with the duct tape prom outfit, suppose you want to make one entirely from scratch? Here's how to make an easy clip-on tie in either a long necktie or bow tie design.

Before you begin:

Follow the instructions on pages 14–15 to make double-sided sheets. For a necktie: 4" x 17" (10 x 43cm), 2¼" x 4½" (5.5 x 11.5cm). For a bow tie: 9" x 2" (23 x 5cm) and 2½" x 1" (6.5 x 2.5cm). Trim the sheets into the necessary shapes as shown in the illustration. Don't worry too much about cutting the curves on the necktie knot just right; just a slight curve along the top and bottom edges will help achieve the conical shape needed.

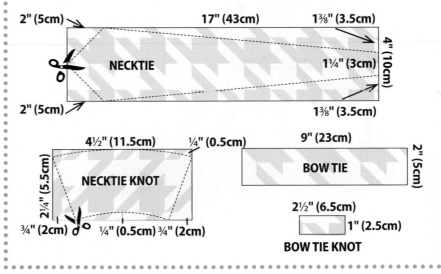

For the bow tie:

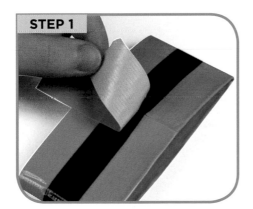

STEP 1

Create the bow. Tape the short ends of the bow tie piece together, creating a loop. Flatten the loop with the seam in the back center.

STEP 2

Add the knot. Pinch the bow tie piece in the center, and then wrap the knot piece around it. Tape the knot piece in place.

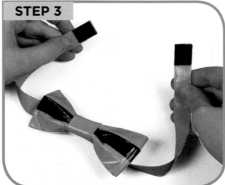

STEP 3

Add the neck strap. For a bow tie neck strap, follow the instructions on page 17 to create a ⅝" (1.5cm)-wide strap the length of your neck circumference + 1" (2.5cm). Tape the bow in place on the center of the strap. Then attach hook-and-loop tape to each end of the strap. Press the hook-and-loop tape in place using the technique on page 12.

For the necktie:

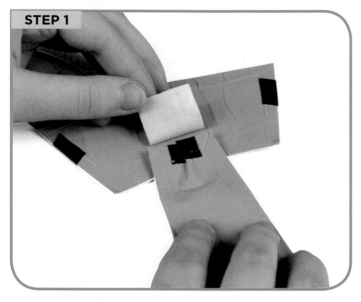

Attach the necktie to the knot. Tape the top narrow end of the necktie to the bottom curved edge of the knot piece.

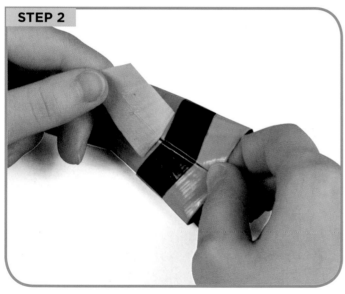

Close up the knot. Bring the short ends of the knot together at the back of the tie, forming a loop. Then tape the ends together to secure them.

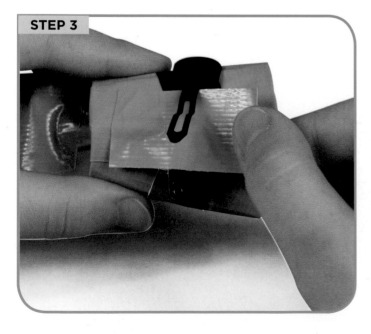

Attach the clip. Tape the large side of the hair clip to the back of the knot to finish for a clip-on tie.

Upcycled Wrist Cuff

Makes: One cuff, sized to the dimensions of your water bottle

Materials & Tools
- Duct tape
- Cutting kit (see page 11)
- Small water bottle (14–18 oz.)
- Brads (optional)

Water bottles are everywhere, it seems, and they pile up faster than you can recycle them. So why not upcycle a few into awesome wrist cuffs? They look great with loads of trimmings—like brads as faux studs—and fit everybody!

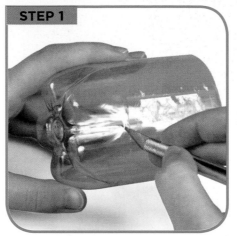

STEP 1

Cut the water bottle. Cut off the top and bottom of your water bottle, leaving just the center flat portion. Start by cutting a slit with your craft knife, then trim off the ends with scissors. You will be left with a tube of plastic.

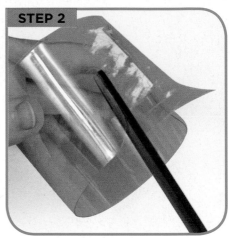

STEP 2

Cut the opening. Cut the tube open so you can slide the cuff on and off your wrist. Round off the cut edges with your scissors.

STEP 3

Cover the plastic with a sheet. To cover the plastic cuff, you have two options. First is to use a sheet of tape. Lay out the sheet (sticky side up). Then center the cuff on top and flatten it out to each side smoothly. Finish the edges as described in the two-sided sheet technique on pages 14–15. Repeat to cover the other side.

STEP 4

Cover the plastic with strips. Alternatively, you can use several strips placed vertically over the cuff to cover the area with more ease and create an interesting striped effect.

STEP 5

Add the brads. Poke holes in the cuff with your craft knife and install brads as desired. Remember to cover the prongs with tape when finished.

Wallet

Makes:

One 4¼" x 3⅜" (11 x 8.5cm) bi-fold wallet

Materials & Tools

- Duct tape in 2–3 colors
- Cutting kit (see page 11)
- 4" x 2½" (10 x 6.5cm) piece of report cover plastic

This handy wallet holds cash and your ID and even has a few slots for cards. It's the perfect and classic wallet with a twist. Add some woven strips of duct tape for a great finishing touch, or make duct tape stickers to turn it into a bacon billfold!

STEP 1

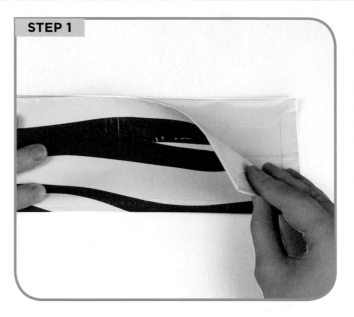

Fold the main wallet. Measure down 3 ⅜" (8.5cm) from one long edge of the wallet. Then fold the wallet lengthwise along this line. One side should be slightly higher than the other; this will be the bill slot once both ends are taped.

STEP 2

Edge the ID pocket. Fold a ½" (1.5cm)-wide strip of duct tape in half over one long end of your ID pocket piece.

STEP 3

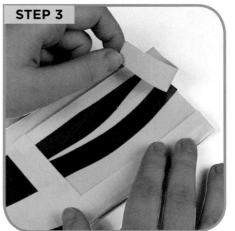

Apply the ID pocket. Place the ID pocket piece on the inner side of your wallet, aligning the right and bottom edges. Tape the pocket in place along the sides and bottom with ½" (1.5cm)-wide strips of tape. Tape around the entire right end of the wallet as you do this to finish one end of the bill slot.

STEP 4

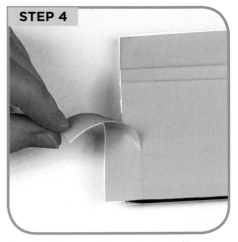

Apply the card pockets. Align the left edge of one card pocket with the left edge of the wallet, about ¾" (2cm) down from the top edge. Tape the pocket in place along the bottom edge only. Attach the second pocket ½" (1.5cm) down from the first, now taping along the sides and bottom. Tape around the entire left end of the wallet as you do this to finish the left end of the bill slot. Use more ½" (1.5cm)-wide strips of tape to decorate the front of the wallet.

Before you begin:

Follow the instructions on pages 14–15 to make three double-sided sheets in the following sizes: one 9" x 6 ½" (23 x 16.5cm), two 4" x 2" (10 x 5cm).

4" (10cm)

2½" (6.5cm)

ID POCKET

4" (10cm)

2" (5cm)

CARD POCKET X2

9" (23cm)

6½" (16.5cm)

WALLET

FOLD LINE

Flip-Flops

Makes: One pair of sandals sized to fit your feet

Materials & Tools
- Duct tape
- Cutting kit (see page 11)
- About 12" x 12" (30.5 x 30.5cm) of cardboard (depending on your shoe size)

These simple but stylish sandals are given a twist (literally) with a strap covered with twisted strips of duct tape. They'll keep your feet airy but still secure on a warm summer day. You can also create a flat or woven strap for a different look to suit your mood.

Before you begin:

Refer to the two-sided duct tape sheet technique on pages 14–15 to cover both sides of the cardboard soles with tape. Follow the instructions on page 17 to create two 2 ½" (6.5cm)-wide straps the length of your instep + 1" [2.5cm]). For the twisted version, make eight ⅝" x 2 ½" (1.5 x 6.5cm) strips and four ¾" (2cm)-wide straps the length of your instep + 1" (2.5cm).

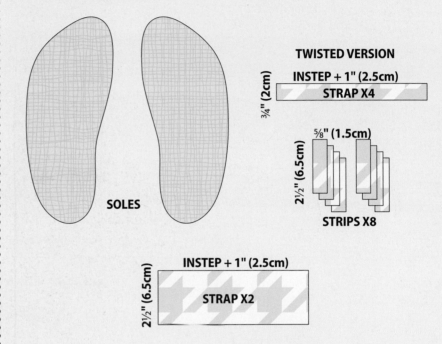

SOLES

TWISTED VERSION

¾" (2cm)

INSTEP + 1" (2.5cm)
STRAP X4

⅝" (1.5cm)

2½" (6.5cm)

STRIPS X8

2½" (6.5cm)

INSTEP + 1" (2.5cm)
STRAP X2

For the soles:

For the sole of your sandal, trace the outline of each foot onto cardboard.

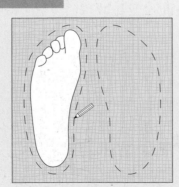

For the straps:

Measure over your instep to determine the length you need for the strap.

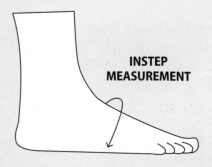

INSTEP MEASUREMENT

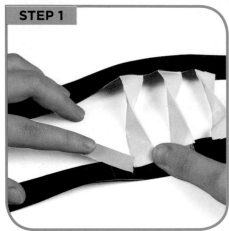

For the twisted version: Create the twists. Take four of the small strips and place one end of each strip on one of the long straps, spacing them about ½" (1.5cm) apart. Tape the strips in place. Twist the free end of each strip 180 degrees and tape it in place on another strap piece. Repeat for the second strap.

Apply the strap. Tape the strap in place on the sole by folding the ends under the sandal by ½" (1.5cm) or so. Try it on and adjust the tape as necessary for the best fit.

WOVEN STRAP

Weave the strap. For a woven version, create three ⅝" (1.5cm)-wide horizontal strips the length of your instep + 1" (2.5cm). Then create vertical strips that are ⅝" (1.5cm) wide and 2½" (6.5cm) long. Create as many vertical strips as needed to cover the length of your horizontal strips. Follow the technique on page 29 to weave the strips together; attach the strap as in Step 2.

Zipper Belt

Makes:
One belt sized to fit your buckle and waist

Materials & Tools
- Duct tape
- Cutting kit (see page 11)
- Cardboard (see measurements for precise quantities)
- Separating zipper (see measurements for precise length; you can buy more than one and piece them together if necessary)
- Stapler
- Belt buckle
- Leather hole punch (optional)

You'd think a belt would be as simple and boring as it gets for a duct tape project, but take a second look! This belt is made with an eye-catching zipper trim that takes it way beyond the ordinary. Together with the buckle of your choosing, you have a real statement piece that can finish off any outfit!

Before you begin:

Cut a cardboard rectangle equal to your belt width x belt length and round off one end. Refer to the two-sided duct tape sheet technique on pages 14–15 to cover both sides of the cardboard with tape.

WAIST + 8" (20.5cm)

BUCKLE WIDTH - ⅜" (1cm)   BELT

ZIPPER: WAIST + 5" (12.5cm)

STEP 1

Apply the extensions. Steps 1–3 are done in small sections for ease. Starting at the rounded end, apply a 10" (25.5cm)-long piece of tape to the back of the belt, overlapping one long edge by about ½" (1.5cm).

STEP 2

Apply the zipper. Trim the zipper slider and other bits off the zipper tape. Flip the belt over and apply one half of the zipper to the sticky portion of the tape so just the zipper teeth overlap onto the front of the belt.

Measure your buckle

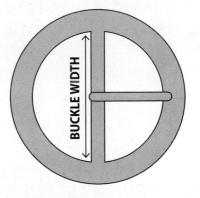

BUCKLE WIDTH

Measure the center bar of your buckle and subtract ⅜" (1cm); this is your belt width. Measure around your waist where you want the belt to lie; add 8" (20.5cm) to get your belt length. Add 5" (12.5cm) to your waist measurement to get the zipper length.

STEP 3

Cover the zipper tape. Fold the exposed portion of tape over onto the zipper so only the zipper teeth are exposed. When finished, repeat Steps 1–3 to continue applying the zipper along that side of the belt for the entire length.

STEP 4

Staple the zipper. Staple the tape-covered zipper in place along the length of the belt. Apply the staples fairly close to the zipper teeth, about ⅛" (0.3cm) away.

STEP 5

Flip and tape the zipper. Fold the zipper over to the back of the belt so only the zipper teeth extend beyond the edge. Tape the zipper in place on the back of the belt, covering the exposed staples. Repeat Steps 1–5 on the other edge of the belt.

STEP 6

Cut the buckle hole. Cut a hole for your buckle tine centered along the width of belt right where the zipper tape ends on the squared end. Start with something like ⅛" x ¼" (0.3 x 0.5cm). Test the fit and cut the hole bigger as needed.

STEP 7

Install the buckle. Push the tine up through the hole and wrap the squared end of your belt around the center bar. Tape the squared end to the back of your belt to secure it.

STEP 8

Cut the belt holes. Cut holes at the rounded end of the belt as necessary for the fit you need. Mine are spaced 2" (5cm) apart and made with a hole punch designed for leather, but a craft knife will also do just fine.

Messenger Bag

Makes:
One 12″ x 9″ (30.5 x 23cm) bag

Materials & Tools
- Duct tape in 1–3 colors
- Cutting kit (see page 11)
- Three empty duct tape rolls
- 4″ x 4″ (10 x 10cm) piece of heavy cardboard
- Stapler
- 3″ (7.5cm) of adhesive-backed hook-and-loop tape
- 20 brads

Before you begin:

Follow the instructions on pages 14–15 to make double-sided sheets in the following sizes: one 12″ x 18″ (30.5 x 45.5cm), one 12″ x 9″ (30.5 x 23cm), one 5 ½″ x 11″ (14 x 28cm), two 9″ x 4″ (23 x 10cm), one 4″ x 12″ (10 x 30.5cm), one 45″ x 2″ (114.5 x 5cm).

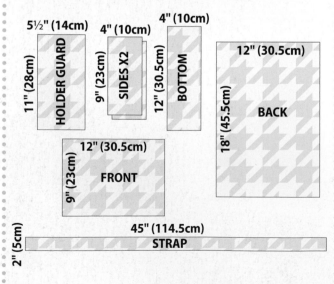

This messenger bag comes equipped with a bottle holder made from all your leftover duct tape rolls! The added caution tape motif on the flap is also perfect for anyone with some rebellious tendencies. Brads act as studs and lend extra strength to the strap and bottle holder while also adding a bit of shine. Because duct tape repels water, this bag is perfect for the gym or beach with a refreshing drink ready to go!

Create the box shape. Follow the instructions on page 16 to create a box from the bottom, front, back, and side pieces. Attach the side, front, and back pieces to the bottom and then fold these pieces up and tape the corners together. This creates a rectangular bag with a flap formed by the extended portion of the back piece.

STEP 2

Assemble the bottle holder. Trace an empty duct tape roll onto the heavy cardboard and cut out the circle. Tape the circle to the bottom of an empty roll. Stack two empty tape rolls on top of the first and cover them in duct tape to hold them all together.

STEP 3

Attach the bottle holder. Tape the bottle holder to one side of the bag along the bottom and inside top edge. Wrap the holder guard around the bottle holder and tape it in place. Five brads on each side of the guard add some extra security if desired.

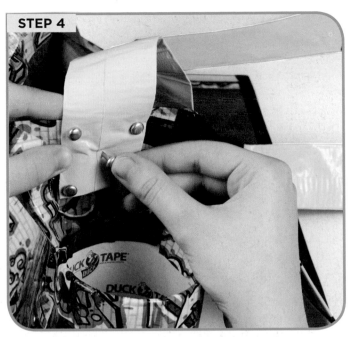

STEP 4

Attach the strap. Center one end of the strap on the top edge of one side panel. Make sure the end of the strap is pointing down toward the bottom of the bag. Use five brads to attach the strap for extra strength. Cover the exposed prongs on the inside of the bag. Repeat on the other side of the bag.

STEP 5

Add the hook-and-loop tape. Attach the hook side of the hook-and-loop tape to the underside of the flap, centered about 1″ (2.5cm) from the edge. Attach the loop side to the front of the bag, centered about 4½″ (11.5cm) down from the top edge.

index